# Hamsa the Butterfly

by Oshri Liron Hakak

BUTTERFLYON BOOKS

First Edition
Copyright ©2023, by Oshri Liron Hakak
All Rights Reserved

Hamsa the Butterfly
Art and Words by Oshri Liron Hakak

Published by Butterflyon Books
Los Angeles
ISBN 979-8-9868755-5-2

For Naksh, and for all of us who are committed
to breathing humanity into flight.

Together, may we release ourselves from the grip of our collective shadow, one breath at a time.

Hamsa the Butterfly

Hamsa crawled up the tree's great trunk.

"Have some leaves, Hamsa— I have plenty of them for you to eat," said the tree.

The leaves gave Hamsa
a kind of nourishment
she didn't even know she needed.

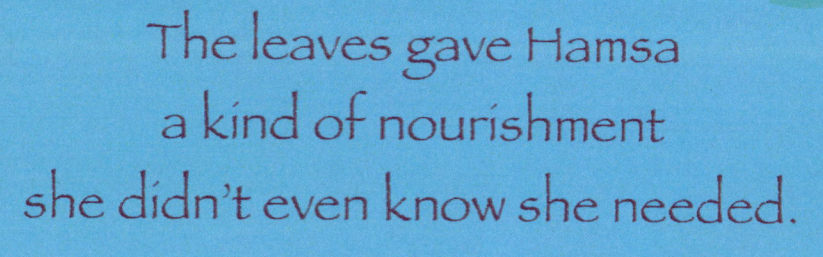

And the tree taught her a song...

"Long, deep breathing makes me brave
when I'm in my shadowy cave.
I breathe out fear and breathe in care,
my wings grow for my heart to dare."

"But, tell me… how is this connected with me flying?" asked Hamsa.

"Soon, you'll see," said the tree.
"For now, I'm going to give you some deep breaths.
Your job is to take them.
And I'll take everything you breathe out.
Okay?"

"Okay," said Hamsa, taking a deep breath.

So Hamsa breathed in and out,
and was able to make something
she had never made before.
She made a thread of silk.

"Keep going…" said the tree.
"Can you make your breaths even slower, and even deeper?"

"Okay," said Hamsa, taking a chance and resting on the thread she had connected to the tree, the thread that she had made with her longer, deeper breaths.

Hamsa kept breathing and kept making threads. It made her feel safe, with the threads holding her as she swung in the air, and she was grateful. She wasn't yet flying, but this was closer.

Hamsa felt snuggly in the cocoon she was weaving.

The wind, so happy to watch Hamsa and the tree connecting as they were, wanted Hamsa and the tree to have an even stronger bond.
So the wind blew its powerful breath onto Hamsa, and Hamsa used her long, deep breaths to make her connection with the tree even stronger.

Now, Hamsa was totally cocooned.
Her breaths became so slow and so deep, they were hardly noticeable.
And at the same time, her breaths were almost the only thing she noticed.
Because all around her, now, and all she could see…

…was her shadow.

Hamsa felt sadness and madness and scaredness, seeing only her shadow.
But she found that when she kept breathing long and deep, she felt better.

Then she remembered the song of the tree:

"Long, deep breathing makes me brave
when I'm in my shadowy cave.
I breathe out fear and breathe in care,
my wings grow for my heart to dare."

The wind blew again
to test the strength of Hamsa's connection with the tree.
Tucked away in her cocoon, all Hamsa could do now was feel it.
But her bond with the tree did not break.

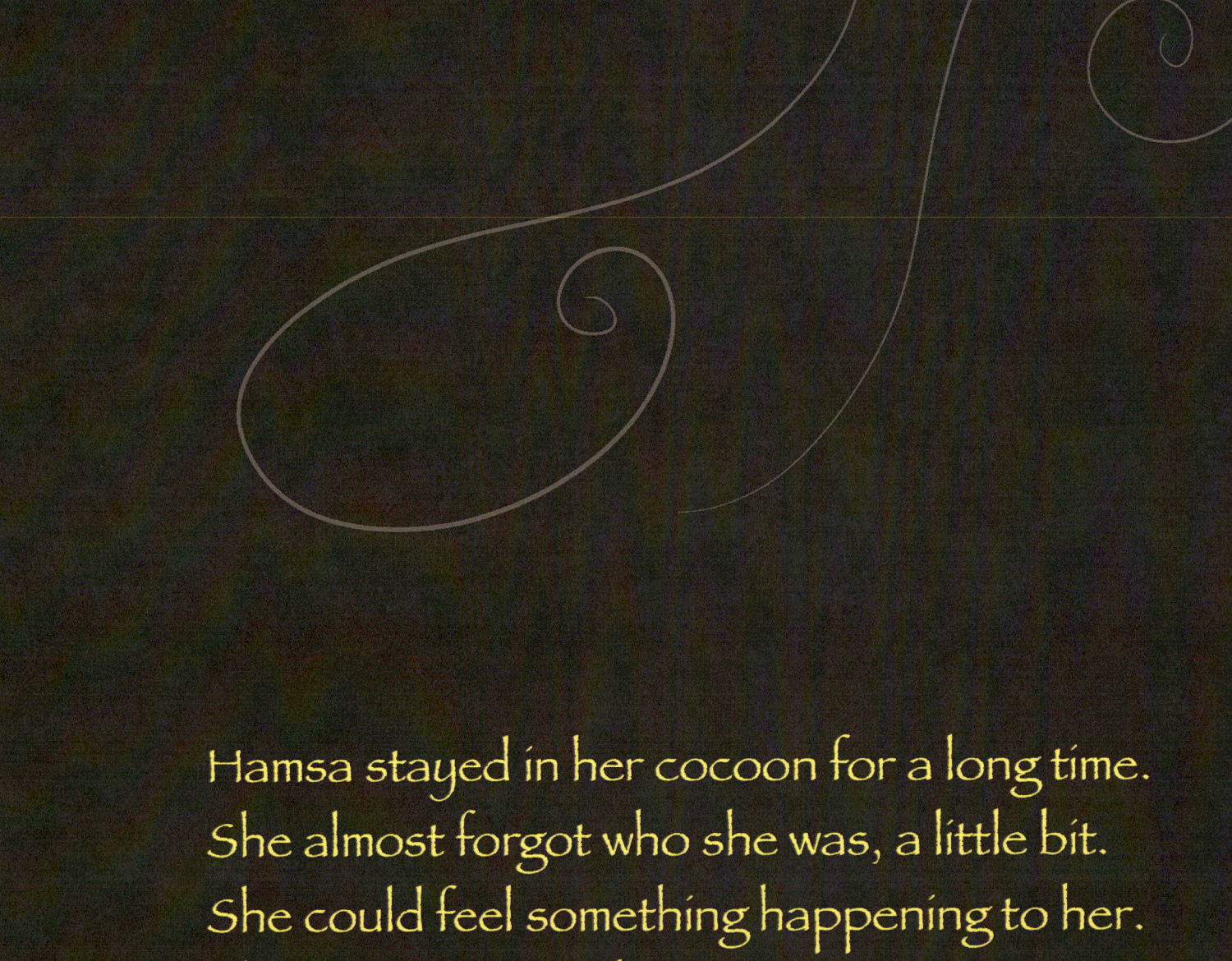

Hamsa stayed in her cocoon for a long time.
She almost forgot who she was, a little bit.
She could feel something happening to her.
She was not sure what.

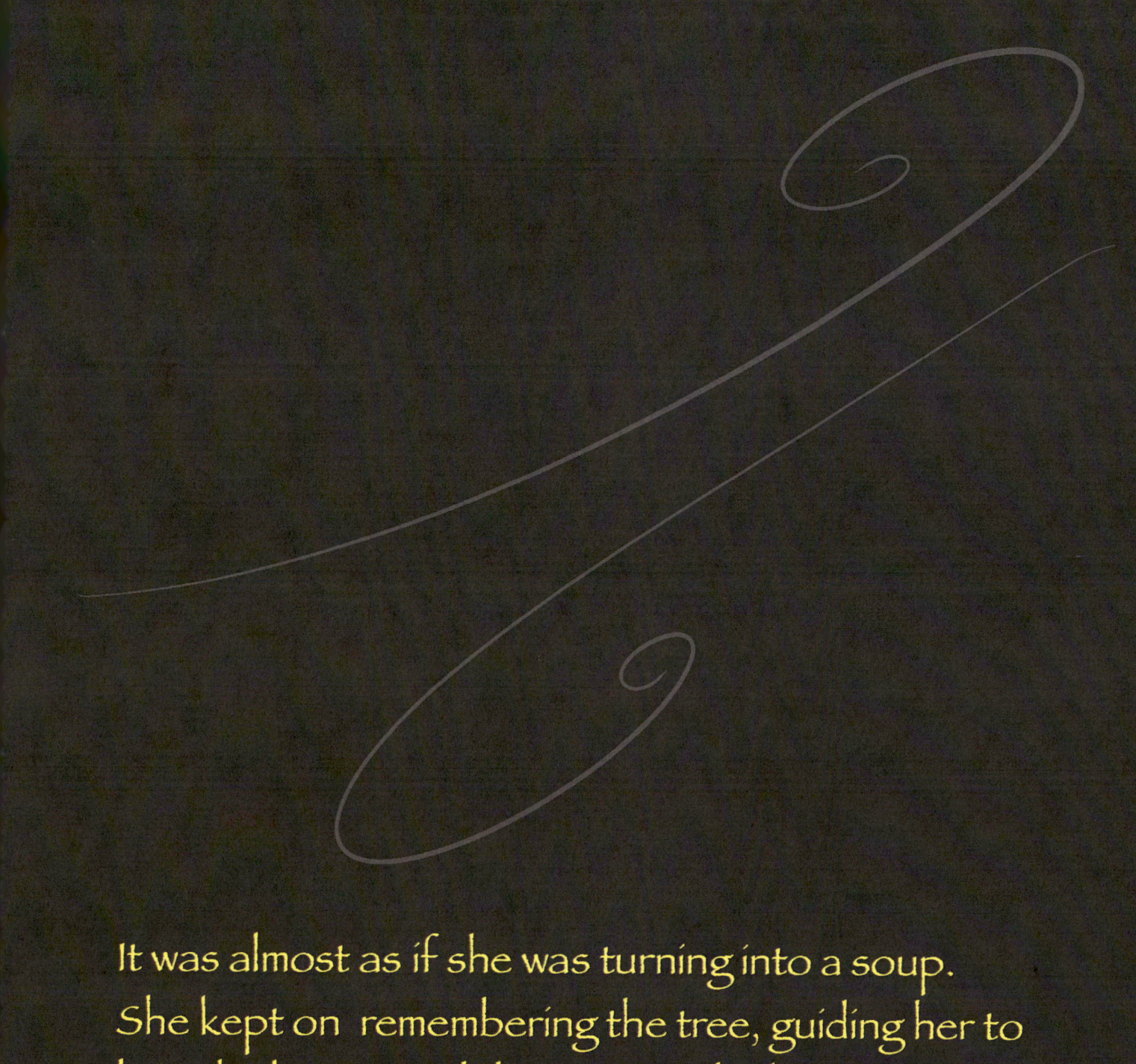

It was almost as if she was turning into a soup.
She kept on remembering the tree, guiding her to
breathe longer and deeper. So she kept going.

One day, Hamsa saw something that she hadn't in a very long time…

It was a single ray of light.

It was time for Hamsa to begin to emerge.
She wasn't yet sure what she had become.

Her cocoon began to open, as she stretched into her new self...

A wing burst out of her cocoon…

Then, for the first time, she flew!

Flying up to the sky, Hamsa sang a song to the tree…

I have breathed… and I have grieved…
I have cooled the rage that in me seethed.
All life is under my protection,
As I commit to the way of deep compassion.
When I see one creature against another,
I guide them to harmony with each other.
The unseen wind supports my flight,
I angle, and it upholds my gentle light.
I breathe slowly, deeply, as I glide,
I'm powerfully carried on my earthly ride.
My bond to you, tree, is now forever.
I will always feel our love's tender tether.

the

bend

Questions for Cacoontemplation…

What is something I'd like to do that feels impossible?

How am I already perfect? (What things do I appreciate about myself most?)

What or who are sources of support in my life?

What are some "juicy leaves" that I feel like might help me prepare to go into a cocoon to transform into my next stage of life?
(For example… safety or courage or patience.)

What in the world might I like to see transform?

How does my own transformation relate to transformation in the world?

What are some of my own shadows? (For example, things about myself that are harder for me to love.)

What does it feel like to accept my shadow? How is it brave?

How can I acknowledge my shadow without feeling like it is all of me?

# Guided Meditation for Protection

Sit comfortably and start to breathe long and deep.

With every breath, expand your sensation of feeling protected.

Start with yourself.

Extend the feeling to people you know and care about.

Extend the feeling now to people who you do not know personally.

Extend the feeling to the planet, offering your energy of care as a gift of protection to the world.

# Guided Meditation for Growing Through a Cocoon

Sit comfortably and start to breathe slowly and deeply.

With every breath, imagine that you are weaving your cocoon around you.

Feel the warmth and safety of your cocoon.

Now, allow yourself to see all the shadowiness of your cocoon.

Whatever becomes visible in the shadow, breathe long and deep with it.

Take as much time as you need.

Observe and experience any shifts, however tiny, that you experience in your cocoon.

Gradually allow yourself to emerge from your cocoon, continuing to breathe long and deep.

# Guided Meditation for Connecting With Our Ancestors and Future Generations (Intended for Groups)

Sit comfortably and start to breathe slowly and deeply.

Scan your body for tensions, as you continue your slow, deep breathing.

With every breath, expand your sensation of protection and support.

Gradually, extend your sense of care, compassion, and support to everyone present. Marinate in the sensation that everyone present supports you, and that you support everyone present.

Extend this sensation to your ancestry, as you continue to breathe slowly and deeply. Feel the sensation of your ancestors supporting you, and supporting everyone in the room. Now allow yourself to experience a sensation of your ancestors supporting everyone else's ancestors, and everyone else's supporting your ancestors and you.

Continue to breathe slowly and deeply. Now invite the sensation of what it feels like for you to support your future generations in the best way possible. Extend that feeling to the future generations of everyone present. Feel that everyone present also draws on their highest capacity to support and care for your own future generations. Invite all the ancestors to also participate in this support for the future generations and children of all present.

Breathing slowly and deeply, now invite the sensation of a hug from everyone present, all their ancestors and your ancestors, and all members of future generations. Marinate in this sensation of being hugged and cared for, for as long as you would like, continuing to breathe slowly and deeply.

## Why Hamsa?

The Hamsa has been a symbol of protection in many spiritual traditions across the world, for thousands of years.

## Thank You NAMI Westside Los Angeles

Thank you to NAMI Westside Los Angeles for supporting the creation of this book. NAMI Westside Los Angeles is a part of NAMI, a grassroots mental health advocacy organization that offers free education, programming and support for people who are struggling with mental health conditions, as well as for those who are supporting loved ones experiencing challenging mental health conditions.

Mental health for anyone is good for everyone. No matter who you are and where you are, you are not alone. You can find out more about NAMI and its offerings at NAMIWLA.org.

# Gratitude

Thank you to my friend, Cecilia Vinkel,
for helping to inspire this book.

## About the Author

Oshri loves to make art, music and books to aid people and communities in our individual and collective healing journey.

You can find more of Oshri's books on ButterflyonBooks.com . His art and music are on instagram— @oshrihakak .

# More titles by Butterflyon Books:
## ButterflyonBooks.com

### Books for 12 Years Old and Up

  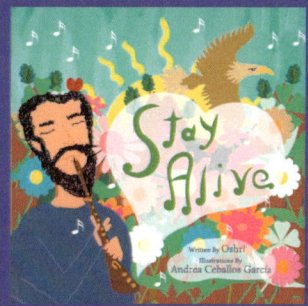 

### Children's Books for All Ages

  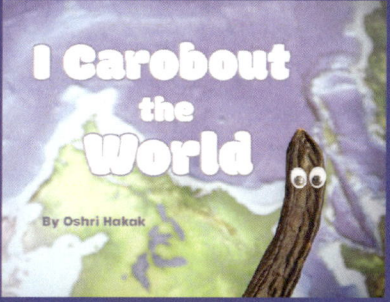 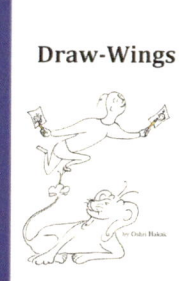

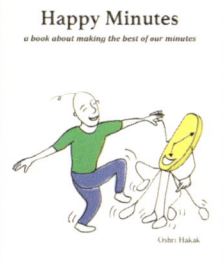 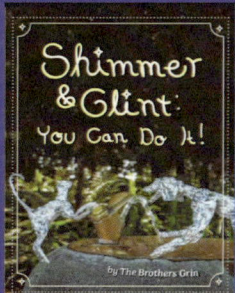 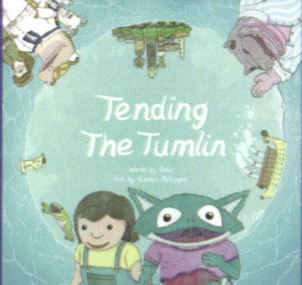  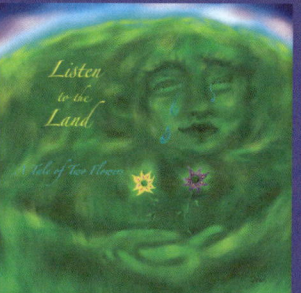

www.ingramcontent.com/pod-product-compliance
Lightning Source LLC
LaVergne TN
LVRC080725070526
838199LV00042B/736